I LOVE TO TRY NEW HAIRSTYLES

MY HAIR IS
BEAUTIFUL

MY CURL PATTERN IS GORGEOUS

I FEEL CONFIDENT WEARING MY HAIR IN ANY STYLE

I LOVE LEARNING ABOUT MY HAIR

MY CURLS
ARE POPPIN

TAKING CARE OF MY HAIR IS IMPORTANT TO ME

MY HAIR IS BEAUTIFUL IN ANY LENGTH SHORT OR LONG

MY
HAIR
IS HEALTHY

MY HAIR
GROWS TOWARDS
THE SUN

I LOVE THE WAY MY HAIR GROWS NATURALLY

I LOVE MY CURLS

MY HAIR IS UNIQUE
AND
UNLIKE ANYONE
ELSE

I LOVE MY HAIR TEXTURE

I LOVE MY LOCS

MY HAIR IS PERFECT BECAUSE IT'S MINE

I SHOW MY HAIR LOVE

I DON'T LET ANYONE TOUCH MY HAIR UNLESS I SAY IT'S OKAY

MY HAIR IS MY CROWN

I LOVE
MY BRAIDS

Made in the USA
Columbia, SC
12 November 2024

46155227R00046